CAPTCHA

Alan Chelak

Image 34 # 9

Image 34 Poetry Series

©2015 Alan Chelak
ISBN-13: 978-1-312-98314-4

1995 *craft*

cainalst are *oody-od* and *craft*
borng and *assel* curved

enter
the great

expOri
distinguish double

swollen
notions swollen
swollen
and
had æra
sslfeaker *entrauth*
nrvised 1995
donastoc *craft*

Please Prove That You Are Human:

shout enter   and

                    was

pepper

                              net

artsy

                    interdicting

tassel

                                   curved   Guru

character

                                        revised

                                                      double

              and   oomph

Cryptoprevent

Moment that horrifies

the only moving picture toobuSy

to ENFORCE their

orders

THE

depository doorway

The

corner of elm

& HUSTON ST.
aslow motion
BLOW UP & The
president'scar

going into
the UNDER pass
WitNessES Gather in

in the

the parkinglot

the image ofhim smiling
& the image ofhim
waving
are
burned
of
course
into the memory

Dowson

ahendil   osubleo

nencionne   uisistra

eckposyc   riganR

againstagainstagainst against
against against against against
against against againstagainst
against against against against
against against against against
against against against against
against against against against
against against againstagainst

moreuki could

character

ceinalst ceinalst
ceinalst ceinalst ceinalst
ceinalst ceinalst ceinalst
ceinalst ceinalst
ceinalst ceinalst
ceinalst
ceinalst

net net net net net net net net net
net net net net net net net net net
net net net net net net net net net
net net net net net net net net net
net net net net net net net net net
net net net net net net net net net
net net net net net net net net net
net net net net net net net net net
net net net net net net net net net
 net net net net net net net net net
net net net net   net   net   net
 net net   net net   net   net
   net   net   net net   net   net
net   net   net net   net net net
   net   net net   net   net net
net   net   net   net   net net net
   net   net net   net   net net

Andy

ina

can of soup

in   acan ofsoup

in acan of soup

inacanofsoup

IN A CAN

OF SOUP

ina can of soup

in A cAn of soup

little   weakling
ubroke me
again

so,

baby was raised
a stillborn

too bored
too strong
baby was
a still born
too bored too
strong

half plaster

cast half

plaster car

halfplasticCARD

halfplastic

identify
popular kids
more crowd
retaining wall
running   up

a   grassy knoll

identify

popular kids

identify

popular kids

identify

popular kids

identify

popular kids

identify

popular kids

came

trembling

like

sea

creatures

I

\ not far from graphic disenchantment of the Gnostic Chum.

It's

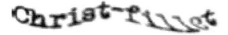

et the controlling belle preserved in a production of enslavement.

I'm

21st certainty wound is based to produce gnostic disillusionment.

REcovery

Now

now i
have everything
well i like to go
for a swim 'cause
i'm goin' nowhere
soon in the snow
or rain or sun
i know i can't be
undone
& now i have
everything

& now i have
everything

& now i have
everything

& now i have
everything

there's

a reson for it

& i'mcrushed
you
saw   it

i know it gets
thatway
sometimes
whereyou never
wake up but
know if you
ever wake up
if you ever wake
up
you're mine

it's true

ar

t

i

s

a

for

m

o

f

property

•

Whethe

r

owne

d

an

d

promote

d

a

s

a

n

investment

,

a

civilizin

g

too

l

fo

r

th

e

middl

e

class

,

a

demonstratio

n

o

f

aristocratic

power

34

,

o

r

a

visua

l

guid

e

for

religious

narrative

,

ar

t

ha

s

alway

s

ha

d

a

n

,

eve

r

sinc

e

i

t

cease

d

bein

g

used

for
mystical
purposes

www.ingramcontent.com/pod-product-compliance
Lightning Source LLC
Chambersburg PA
CBHW051217050326
40689CB00008B/1349